MATTHEW MEAD
Christmas All Through the House

FOUNDER, CREATIVE DIRECTOR, EDITOR IN CHIEF
Matthew Mead
MANAGING EDITOR Jennifer Mead
EXECUTIVE EDITOR Linda Bullock
SENIOR EDITOR Sarah Egge
GRAPHIC DESIGNER
Brian Michael Thomas/Our Hero Productions
STUDIO ASSISTANT/DESIGNER Lisa Bisson

Matthew would like to thank everyone who contributed their time, talents, and/or invited us into their homes to help create this special volume, CHRISTMAS ALL THROUGH THE HOUSE: Laurie Carey; Michelle and Gary Coffin and their children; The Courser family of Courser Farm; Lisa Fantasia at Wicked Unique Cakes and Treats; Joanne Grenon at Grenon Trading Company; Ryan Linehan at The Kimball-Jenkins Estate; Bethany Lowe and her team; Marie and Everett Mead; Lisa Renauld; Sally Robinson at Fancy Flours; Mary and Gordon Welch; Julie Merberg for her unyielding support; and the hardworking team at Time Home Entertainment, Inc.

OXMOOR HOUSE
EDITORIAL DIRECTOR Leah McLaughlin
CREATIVE DIRECTOR Felicity Keane
BRAND MANAGER Nina Fleishman Reed
SENIOR EDITOR Andrea Kirkland, M.S., R.D.
MANAGING EDITOR Elizabeth Tyler Austin

**MATTHEW MEAD'S
CHRISTMAS ALL THROUGH THE HOUSE**
EDITOR Meredith Butcher
PROJECT EDITOR Emily Chappell Connolly
ASSISTANT DESIGNER Allison Sperando Potter
ASSOCIATE PRODUCTION MANAGER Kimberly Marshall

PUBLISHER Jim Childs
VICE PRESIDENT, BRAND & DIGITAL STRATEGY
Steven Sandonato
EXECUTIVE DIRECTOR, MARKETING SERVICES
Carol Pittard
EXECUTIVE DIRECTOR, RETAIL & SPECIAL SALES
Tom Mifsud
EXECUTIVE PUBLISHING DIRECTOR Joy Butts
**DIRECTOR, BOOKAZINE DEVELOPMENT &
MARKETING** Laura Adam
FINANCE DIRECTOR Glenn Buonocore
ASSOCIATE PUBLISHING DIRECTOR Megan Pearlman
ASSISTANT GENERAL COUNSEL Helen Wan
SPECIAL THANKS Katherine Barnet, Jeremy Biloon, Dana Campolattaro, Susan Chodakiewicz, Rose Cirrincione, Jacqueline Fitzgerald, Christine Font, Hillary Hirsch, David Kahn, Mona Li, Amy Mangus, Nina Mistry, Dave Rozzelle, Ricardo Santiago, Adriana Tierno, Vanessa Wu

ISBN 10: 0-8487-4258-3
ISBN 13: 978-0-8487-4258-4

We welcome your comments and suggestions about Time Home Entertainment Books. Please write to us at: Time Home Entertainment Books, Attention: Book Editors, P.O. Box 11016, Des Moines, IA 50336-1016

If you would like to order any of our hardcover Collector's Edition books, please call us at 1-800-327-6388, Monday through Friday, 7 a.m. to 8 p.m., or Saturday, 7 a.m. to 6 p.m., Central Time.

With any craft project, check product labels to make sure that the materials you use are safe and nontoxic. The instructions in this book are intended to be followed with adult supervision.

NOTE: Neither the publisher nor the author is responsible for your specific health or allergy needs that may require medical supervision, or for any adverse reactions to the recipes contained in this book.

The holiday season is like good news, and it's hard not to spread the word far and wide. So this year, we've focused on ways to broadcast Christmas all through the house. In doing so, we have discovered new ways of extending decorating ideas into parties, gifts, outdoor décor, and fresh traditions.

My personal focus is always on ease, preparedness, and, of course, reusing, recycling, and re-crafting. This volume is filled with all the projects, how-to coaching, and beautiful inspiration you'll need to engage in and enjoy every moment of this fleeting time.

We hope they will carry you though the year with fond memories—and help you anticipate the next season.

From my family to yours,
Merry Christmas!

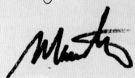

MATTHEW MEAD
Christmas All Through the House

THROW A FUN
Snowman Party

EVERYONE'S FAVORITE ICON OF WINTER INSPIRES THE TREATS AND DÉCOR OF THIS YOUTHFUL PARTY.

Make memories that will melt your heart.

Snowmen are lucky, no one watches their waistlines—the rounder the better. Tap into that carefree attitude to stage a dessert-focused party that features this friendly seasonal celebrity. Stage it during a snow day or a weekend afternoon, and invite anyone of any age who wants to get into a festive spirit—and maybe get a little frosting on their fingers, too. All the fixings are easy to acquire at grocery, dollar, and crafts stores.

Wrapped gift boxes can be used for decoration or for guests to take away (RIGHT). Fill the boxes with dollar-store games, then top with a woolen glove stuffed with treats. Purchase or make chocolate cupcakes, and top them with snow-white frosting. Use colored fondant to form snowman features for the tops (BOTTOM RIGHT). Fill a carafe with refreshing milk, then tie a scarf around the neck (BOTTOM LEFT).

Transform plain glass plates into themed-dinnerware using your printer and double-stick tape. Print text in color, then cut it out in a circle small enough to fit the bottom of the plate. Adhere with tape. Learn how to embellish the cookies on page 16.

Matthew Mead

friendly faces

These edible ideas set the scene for the party: **1.** For a sweet take on chips and dip, dish up a bowl of whipped cream or white chocolate mousse and dust it with orange sprinkles. Offer marshmallows and crisp cookies to enjoy with it. **2.** A bowl of mini-marshmallows goes fast. Affix paper printed with a seasonal word or saying to the bottom of the glass container using double-stick tape. **3.** By letting the treats form the bulk of the décor, you don't have to invest in specialty linens, platters, or decorations. Basic white cake stands, a tablecloth of red-striped linen, and orange ornaments underscore the simple color palette.

OPPOSITE: Decorate a large glass canister or jar with features cut from colored paper and adhered with double-stick tape. Load it with jumbo marshmallows, and turn over a large crockery platter or plate as a hat. A scarf completes the frosty attire.

snowflake

Crafting a
SNOWMANGLASS

What you'll need:

- ○ Candy melts in orange and black, which you can find in the cake and cookie decorating section of a crafts store or online from Wilton.com
- ○ Clean, new paintbrush
- ○ Clear glasses
- ○ Stirring spoon
- ○ Striped party straws

ONE: Gather your supplies. Then, according to package directions, melt the candy coating and stir until smooth. In a microwave, you do this by heating the melts at 40-percent power (or the defrost setting) for 1 minute. Then stir and heat again at 30-second intervals until most of the candy has melted.

TWO: Use the paintbrush to apply the melted candy to the inside of the glass.

THREE: Allow the face to dry completely before filling the glass with cold milk. A hot beverage will cause the face to melt off the glass. Serve with party straws.

HOW TO POPCORN BALLS

WHAT YOU'LL NEED: Store-bought kettle corn, plastic wrap pieces measuring 12x10 inches, black and orange colored paper, scissors, hot-glue gun

STEP BY STEP:

ONE: Scoop handfuls of kettle corn into each piece of plastic wrap and twist to form a ball shape. Secure ends of plastic wrap with hot glue if needed.

TWO: Cut small carrot noses and black eyes and mouth pieces from paper. Use hot-glue gun to adhere to the plastic-wrapped ball.

This no-cook method is perfect for young children. But older kids can make these sticky, sweet treats using a favorite popcorn balls recipe.

Display the treats in an eye-catching way, such as inside this wire Christmas tree form, or piled inside a costume top hat.

Crafting
SMILINGSNOWMEN

What you'll need:

- ○ Food-safe markers (also called edible markers) in orange and black from the cookie-decorating aisle of the crafts store or online at Wilton.com

- ○ White-frosted cookies, such as these pfeffernüsse cookies from the grocery store

- ○ Large marshmallows

- ○ Bamboo skewers

- ○ Small twigs

- ○ Square of rigid foam (optional)

ONE: Array the cookies on a cooling rack, then use the markers to draw on features.

TWO: Each cookie has a different face, and when you let children get into the act of drawing on faces, the expressions get even wackier and more fun.

THREE: In the same manner as the cookies, use the markers to draw faces on marshmallows.

FOUR: Stack two or three marshmallows using a bamboo skewer through the center to hold them together. Cut the skewer to length, and anchor it in a piece of foam if needed for stability. Poke in small, skinny twigs for arms.

Wrap ROOM

SET UP A DEDICATED SPACE TO EASE THE PRESENT-WRAPPING RUSH.

Include the supplies to make unique tags and embellishments.

Any creative hobby, from painting to scrapbooking to photography, becomes more enjoyable when you have a dedicated space to practice your art. Gift-wrapping is no different. You'll have more fun with this task if you have a spot to store supplies and spread out. So, if you have ever wrapped presents on the washing machine or the guest bed, this is for you. Follow these steps to wrapping bliss:

Step 1—Make room. Erect a table in an out-of-the way corner. If you enjoy wrapping gifts year-round, you might want to make this more than a temporary installation. The work surface could be in a corner of the kitchen, a spare closet or room, or in a re-purposed armoire. If you need an outlet for a glue gun or desk lamp, plan accordingly.

Step 2—Corral supplies. Gather basics like scissors and papers, as well as special trims, glitters, and hole punches. Sort items into jars, baskets, boxes, tins, vases, or whatever makes them accessible and pretty. Remember, this is a spot that's supposed to foster creativity, and that's more likely to happen if the area is clutter-free and attractive.

Step 3—Get started. There are a dozen ideas presented here, and many more inspiring materials and trims.

To keep rolls of paper from getting crushed and wrinkled, hang each roll on a loop of string on the wall (LEFT). The cascade of papers becomes art, and you can quickly cut off the amount you need. To snag this handy utility apron ($35), which is made in the U.S. from all-natural cotton, check out our friend designer Janna Lufkin's site, RawMaterialsDesign.com.

A cotton utility apron has deep pockets to keep a variety of paper-working tools secure and handy. And, tacked to the wall, it doesn't take up room on the work surface.

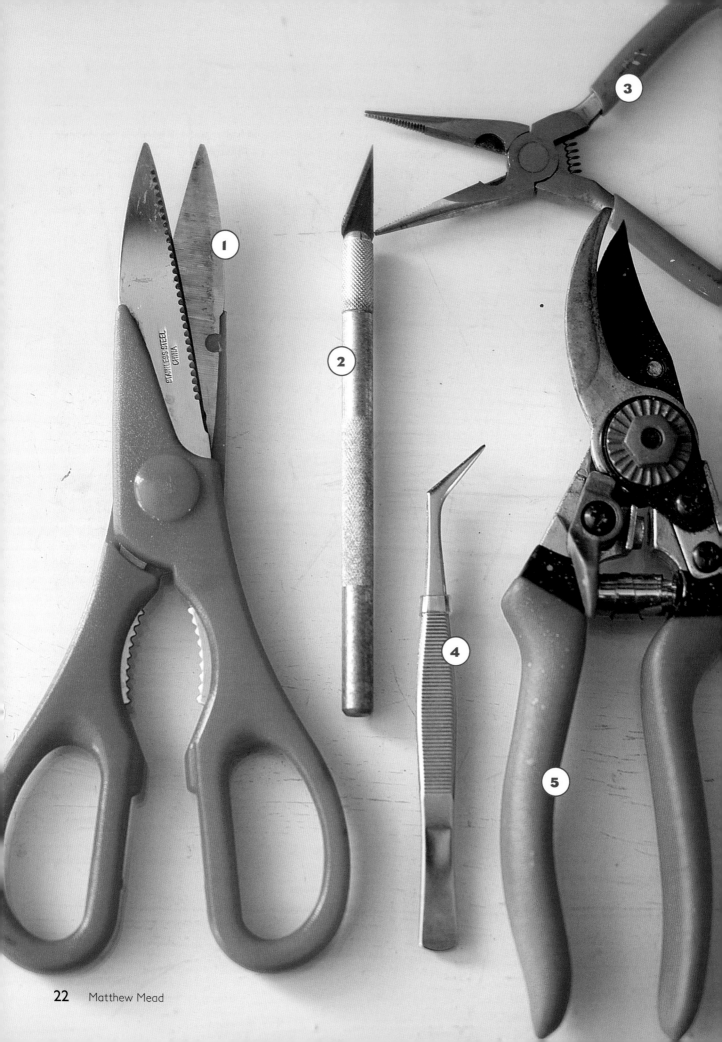

TOOLS & SUPPLIES

You can stock your wrapping space with anything, but here are some general tools you might find helpful: **1.** Kitchen shears help when you're cutting through dense materials like felt and cardboard. **2.** A hobby knife, like this X-ACTO® knife, lets you cut out intricate designs or trace straightedges. **3.** Needle-nose pliers let you grab, twist, and cut wire. **4.** Precision tweezers are excellent at grasping tiny beads or placing a single piece of glitter. **5.** Pruning shears work on live as well as artificial flowers, which make excellent package toppers. **6.** Use baking cups as toppers for jars of ingredients or specialty foods. **7.** Jack-of-all-trade chopsticks can be decorative additions, placeholders, straightedges, or used to coil wire. **8.** Glitters from BethanyLowe.com provide the sparkle that takes a package from drab to fab. **9.** You can purchase ready-made gift tags at the crafts store, or, punch or cut your own from card stock. Make a big batch to keep handy all year.

inspiration points

Let these ideas spark your creativity: **1.** This vintage tin, which Matthew found at a flea market, can be a container for supplies or the wrapping itself. Keep several on hand for gifting baked goods. **2.** Using scrapbook papers, fashion your own tags and cards. **3.** Muffin cups become decorative toppers when you add paper flower stickers. See instructions on page 26. **4.** A stag woodcut inspired Matthew to make woodland-theme cards, using pinecone die-cuts and scalloped scissors to cut rickrack.

unique embellishments

Matthew converted a vintage armoire into a wrapping center, painting the interior red and adding a woodcut motif to the door. This is an excellent small-space solution. You can store extra boxes and tins of supplies on the shelves, lay wrapping paper rolls horizontally, and tuck gift bags and ribbon spools into the drawers.

WHAT YOU'LL NEED: White wrapping paper, red striped scrapbook paper, red wire, chopstick or pencil, double-stick tape, scissors, wire cutters, hot-glue gun, ball ornament, paper flower stickers

STEP BY STEP:

ONE: Wrap package with plain white paper. Gather paper flower stickers and patterned paper.

TWO: Wrap wire around the package three times, then tie off in a simple knot. To add flourish to the cut ends, twist them around a chopstick to make springy coils.

THREE: Use double-stick tape to attach a piece of patterned paper to the top of the package, add flower sticker, and hot-glue on a ball ornament.

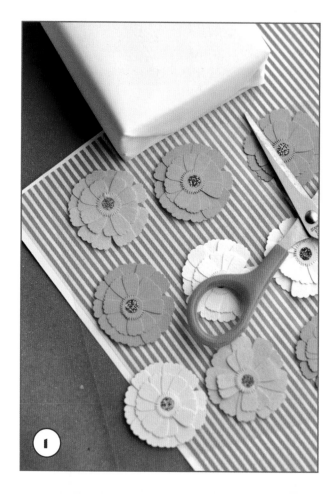

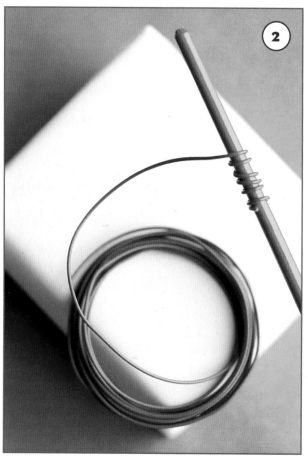

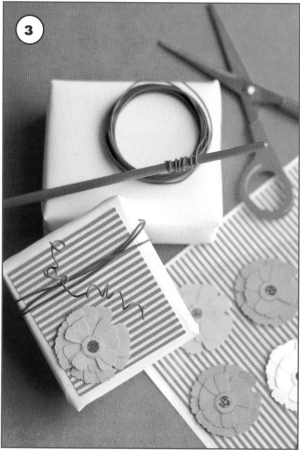

Good
TIDINGS

DRESS UP YOUR GUEST SPACE WITH LAYERS OF SOFTNESS AND LUXURY.

Use thrift-store garments to make these colorful, inventive projects.

Make lavender- or buckwheat-filled sachets scented with essential oils out of the sleeves of a shirt. Hem the bottom, then simply tie closed with ribbon.

Knowing from experience

that traveling during the holidays can be as exhausting as it is rewarding, Matthew and Jenny helped a friend outfit her guest space with cheerful, restorative accoutrements designed to lift the spirits. "We chose bright, engaging colors when we mixed and matched things at the thrift store," Jenny says. In addition to color, they looked for tactile appeal, choosing soft wool sweaters and weathered silk shirts for $2 to $10. The finished hems, collars, and cuffs on the garments helped keep sewing to a minimum. "Once we washed everything, they took hardly any time to make," she says. And the best part: After the visit, friends and family can take home some of the items as memory-filled parting gifts.

Matthew asked his friend Darryl Moland of The Decorated Tree blog to create a tabletop-size decoration (RIGHT). Darryl swirled acrylic paints on the inside of clear glass ornaments to create the punchy color on his slender feather tree available at HomeTraditions.com. Tiny packages placed around the tree base (ABOVE) reinforce the color scheme. They contain luxurious soaps, small shampoos, and bath sprays the guests will find pampering.

To make a sheath for the drum lampshade, Matthew cut away the trunk of a cable-knit sweater, and hot-glued the top and bottom edges to the inside of the shade. Fabric-covered buttons are finishing details.

A variety of wrapped packages make festive decoration for the dresser in a guest's room and set the tone for the holiday celebrations.

little snippets

All you need are some small scraps to make these projects: **1.** Wrap up sweet treats to set on a pillow. **2.** Hang a stocking made from a sweater with a shirting cuff on a dresser knob. Get the template on page 111. **3.** Sweater sleeves snugly fit around jelly jars used as candleholders. **4.** To make an ornament, trace around a cookie cutter and then iron on fusible webbing. Finally, punch a hole for embroidery floss, and hang it from a guest's hanger, bedpost, or suitcase handle.

GUEST BLANKET

WHAT YOU'LL NEED: New or vintage plain blanket with finished edges (this can also be done with fleece blankets that don't fray), yarn, vinyl tape measure, large needle, clothespins or metal hair clips

STEP BY STEP:

ONE: Choose a yarn that is a contrasting shade from the blanket, so this finishing detail is easy to see.

TWO: Clip the tape measure to the edge of the blanket.

THREE: Begin the blanket stitch, which you can imitate from these photos or view on any needlecraft website.

FOUR: Using the table measure as a guide, sew at even intervals.

The blanket stitch is easy enough for a needlework novice—even someone who cannot sew—to accomplish.

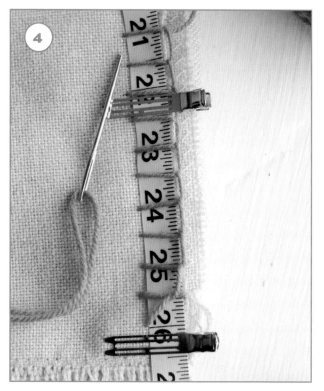

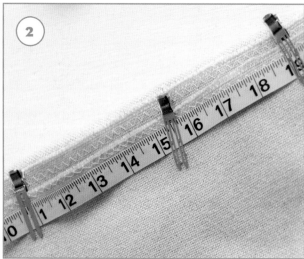

Crafting
SWEATER COZIES

What you'll need:

- ○ Thrift store sweaters and cardigans
- ○ Bolster-pillow form
- ○ Fabric scissors
- ○ Needle and thread
- ○ Satin ribbon
- ○ Hot water bottle

ONE: Choose one-color sweaters in good condition, though you can work around small holes or snags. Wash and line-dry them before use.

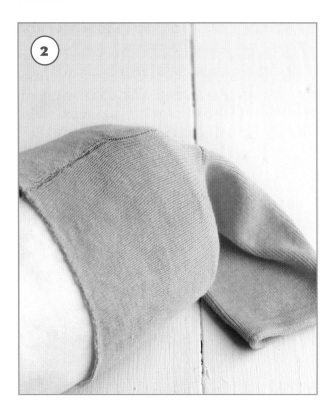

TWO: For the bolster pillow, cut two sleeves from one sweater. Place the sleeves over the end of the pillow form.

THREE: Cut the trunk of a second sweater and use the large square to wrap around the form and cover the cut ends of the sleeves. Hand-sew the seam closed at the back.

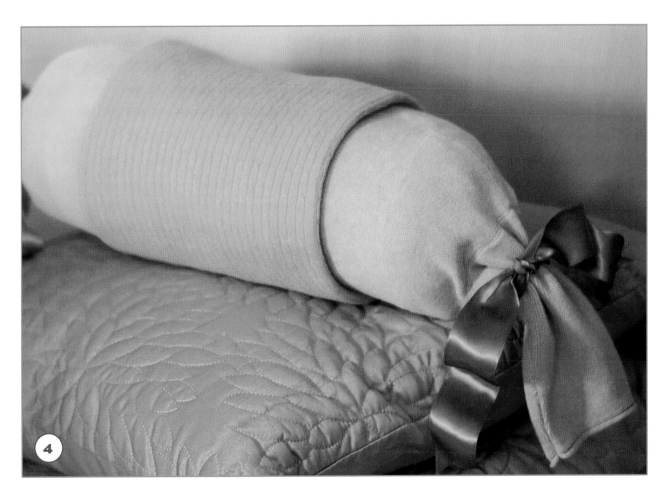

FOUR: Tie the sleeves using satin ribbon in a complementing color.

FIVE: To make a cover for a hot-water bottle, lay a cardigan sweater flat and fasten the buttons up the front. Trace the bottle onto the front, and then cut out through both front and back pieces of the sweater. Use needle and thread to hand-sew the edges. Unfasten the buttons and insert the water bottle. Fill when ready to use.

Fulfill every guest's wish and desire with soft pillows and a hot water bottle tucked between the sheets.

PICTURE
Perfect

PHOTO STYLIST KELLY McGUILL PARES HER HOME DOWN TO JUST THE ESSENTIAL GORGEOUS ELEMENTS.

Learn how she celebrates the holidays in a way that's stylish and meaningful.

Creating a beautiful home

is interior designer Kelly McGuill's specialty. Making it welcoming is where she excels. Her Colonial-style house in the suburbs of Boston is a showcase for her work as a photo stylist. It's full of carefully curated vintage furnishings, injected with lively modern pieces, for an overall look that is sophisticated but comfortable. It's also very neat.

Her home is also where her sisters drop by almost daily for a quick chat, where she plays Monopoly with her nephew at the kitchen table, and where she hosts big potluck suppers with friends. Things also can get very messy.

Kelly is happy with all aspects of her life—the neat and the messy. In fact, the one seems to help the other: Her tidy collections are the same pitchers and platters she fills when friends arrive. She keeps candles and spare glassware in open shelving to create an instant cocktail party mood. The monopoly game gets tucked away in a trunk in the living room—out of sight but ready. "The things I collect, decorate with, and use in my work are also very handy and useful. To me, it's the perfect combination."

An interior designer for many years, Kelly McGuill (ABOVE), branched into photo styling so she could satisfy her love of photography. She places the "props" that make a room aesthetically pleasing for a catalog or magazine. You can see samples of her work at KellyMcGuillHome.com, and read about her adventures in decorating and with her golden retriever, Stella, on her blog KellyMcGuill.blogspot.com.

The palette in her home is soft and muted, and so is her holiday decorating. She plays off the furniture pieces that are natural wood and mid-tone leather to introduce bronze-color ornaments.

time-saving ideas

The holidays can be very busy, particularly when companies hire Kelly to help with seasonal catalog shoots. So she doesn't always put up and decorate a tree. She gains the same fragrance and atmosphere with other greenery, such as window wreaths and centerpiece arrangements. Wrapped packages (**ABOVE**) are placed around the house as decoration instead of corralled under a tree. The papers play off the pear-green colors of her pillows. To get many of her decorations, Kelly just stocks up at the grocery store, filling her basket with Bartlett pears (**RIGHT**) and limes.

OPPOSITE: The living room shows Kelly's preference for breathing room in a home. A cane-seat armchair is lightweight, see-through seating, the windows are uncovered and clean, and the rug is warm and textural, but quietly neutral, in a shade similar to the color of the wood floors.

dinner's ready

Kelly loves to host friends and family at her sizable farm table in the dining room (OPPOSITE). Wicker chairs are vintage, and she added new linen-covered host chairs for an interesting mix. A pretty arrangement of porcelain plates is a subtle backdrop for the food and faces illuminated by candlelight.

THIS PAGE: On one wall, a rustic shelf holds extra dinnerware and pitchers, sorted by size. Kelly prefers natural wood finishes, using the tones of the different species, from oak to maple, as colorful variation in her home's neutral palette.

quick take-away

Kelly has different approaches, depending on the time available. **1.** An arrangement of pears and variegated euonymus leaves in a glass compote comes together in moments. **2.** Place settings are easy to throw together: Meld an ironed napkin with flatware and a small ramekin filled with green snippets. **3.** With more time, Kelly bakes quick breads to give away. (A dash to the bakery also works, too!)

OPPOSITE: Packaged in clear cellophane, the quick bread can anchor a gift basket with a bottle of wine and fresh fruit. Kelly collects white marble slabs, often leftover from broken-down old dressers or tables, to use as pedestals on her tables.

timeless and flexible

By limiting her collections and decorative items to narrow categories (marble, natural wood, old glass, white pottery), Kelly can mix and match items to create endless compositions at home or for work. Large glass jars (**LEFT**) can hold everything from pantry staples to laundry detergent to fresh flowers. A smattering of glittery ornaments (**BELOW**) can be placed next in any of her collections, and they contrast nicely with the rustic wood surfaces. You can learn how to make the ornaments on page 52.

OPPOSITE: This console table grouping makes use of many of Kelly's favorite pieces. It conveys seasonal spirit but in a way that's not tied to the holiday. After the presents are opened, the same elements will be elegant wintertime decoration.

gathering spot

The light and airy kitchen echoes with laughter when Kelly's sisters stop by. At the center of the table—a smaller version of the farm table in her dining room—Kelly laid a boxwood wreath around a candle to create an easy centerpiece. The light fixture looks like a giant ornament.

scenic lookout

Kelly is always on the hunt for old doors and windows. The architectural elements bring grace and patina to a room, and she fashions many into mirrors. Hung in the hallway, this set provides dimension to break up a flat, featureless expanse of wall. An elegant boxwood wreath is a versatile decoration.

HOW TO) GLITTER BULBS

WHAT YOU'LL NEED: Plain ornaments, ModPodge® découpage medium, paint brush, paint markers, various loose glitters (these are from BethanyLowe.com)

STEP BY STEP:

ONE: To cover a portion of an ornament in glitter, first paint on the découpage medium, which will dry clear. While it's still tacky, sprinkle on the glitter, or roll the ornament in a shallow dish filled with glitter.

TWO: To add decorative motifs to the ornaments, purchase white, metallic, or opalescent paint pens, and doodle the designs using straight lines and dots.

THREE: These ornaments work well as a group because the colors—from the ornament finishes, to the glitters, to the paint markers—are consistent.

This is a budget-friendly way to create elegant and unique decorations to use throughout the house.

CHRISTMAS FROM THE
Kitchen

DOWNSHIFT FROM RETAIL THIS YEAR WITH HANDMADE GIFTS.

Invite friends to join you for an afternoon of making goodies.

It's a time-honored tradition to give handmade gifts for the holiday. Family recipe cookies, quick breads, fruitcakes, preserves, and infused spirits all have a special quality that makes them heartfelt presents for loved ones and friends. Preparing and presenting such a gift doesn't have to be as laborious as you might imagine. Matthew has culled a few of the quickest techniques and ready-at-hand ingredients to offer you here. Share the ideas—and your kitchen—with a few friends who love to cook, and you'll have the makings of a lovely get-together, plus some treats to give away.

Prepare by gathering clean glass bottles and canisters. You can buy new canning supplies at hardware and grocery stores, pick up gently used ones at flea markets, or reuse what you have leftover in the recycling bin (OPPOSITE). If you choose the recipes that require canning, such as the brandied pears, the jars will have to be sanitized in boiling water—though that's a good idea for any of the recipes. Make sure everything has a tight-fitting lid. Also gather together the fodder for Matthew's wrapping ideas: scraps of linen, spools of twine, and ribbon snippets. Once you're set, you'll be surprised how quickly and effortlessly these gifts come together.

To make life easier—and cheaper—rely on seasonal ingredients, greenery, and decorations (TOP). Fresh herbs like potted thyme (MIDDLE) and the edible leaves of the bay laurel plant (BOTTOM), which are most fragrant in October, are handy to have around.

cook's lab

Make the kitchen an inviting place to work by de-cluttering countertops and having supplies ready. If you wish, experiment with a few techniques before friends arrive and have them on hand as samples.

pretty delicious

It's hard not to be inspired by
the beauty of a statuesque and
fragrant dwarf evergreen
plant studded with berry
clusters in a large ceramic
pot. Fresh seasonal fruit,
such as pears and figs, are easy to
come by and can trigger delectable
flavor combinations for preserves
and jams.

party planning

Set up the stations for preparing these treats in a kitchen or dining space. Multiple stations means guests won't be bumping into one another—though that's half the fun! Utilize countertops, buffets, tables, and islands. You may need to set up temporary work surfaces, too, such as folding tables, to hold wrapping supplies (RIGHT). Cover non-food-safe surfaces with tablecloths, and keep cutting boards and mixing bowls handy (BELOW).

OPPOSITE: Matthew set up a separate work area on one side of the kitchen, away from the island. Ingredients are in attractive pots and containers, including a stocking sewn from a French tea towel. The doors of the wall cabinet are screened with copies of old handwritten family recipes.

infused vinegars

There's no cooking or canning involved in this appealing gift recipe. To flavor vinegars for dressings and seasonings, place herbs and spices in clean glass bottles, cover completely with white vinegar, and seal tightly with screw-on caps or corks. Bay leaves make for a fragrant arrangement for the kitchen, and they can be added to the vinegars. Once the bottles are sealed, store them in a cool dry place. Make note of the date, because the vinegars won't reach peak flavor for six weeks.

OPPOSITE: Some of Matthew's favorite flavorings for vinegars are peppercorns of all colors; fresh herbs such as thyme, lemon thyme, sage, and oregano; and other aromatics like garlic.

inventory check

Surely you can think of someone who might love to receive each of these foodstuffs: **1.** Homemade coffee liqueur is a useful gift that recipients can enjoy in a cocktail, add to their cup of joe, or mix into baked goods and basting sauces for deep flavor notes. To make it, check out the recipe at HolidayWithMatthewMead.com. **2.** Winter roasting salt, which includes a healthy dose of multicolor peppercorns, will add kick to roasts and root vegetables. **3.** You can preserve sweet peaches and pears, piquant lemons, and savory olives, peppers, and garlic cloves. Look online or in cookbooks for basic canning recipes. You'll find a recipe for preserved lemons on page 71. We also provide a recipe for brandied peaches and pears at HolidayWithMatthewMead.com.

OPPOSITE: Keep things organized by listing flavor combinations, recipe ideas, or a summary of gifts that need decorative wrapping or tags.

1

COFFEE LIQUEUR

2

3

WINTER ROASTING SALT

complete package

Wrappings should be as rustic and old-fashioned as the gifts themselves. Cut linen, burlap, or cheesecloth into small squares in a few different sizes. Fray the raw edges to make fringe, then use the squares as bottle and jar toppers. Secure with velvet or grosgrain ribbons, or nubby string and twine.

OPPOSITE: For an impressive presentation, package several delectable goodies into one container, and tuck in sprigs of berries, fresh bay leaves, or other seasonal greens and fresh fruits. Old grain measures, cheese boxes, and vintage tins with patina on them have the right feel, but you could also use baskets or reusable grocery totes.

Matthew Mead

will work for food

Keep your hardworking guests sated with delicious munchies that carry out the earthy, in-season theme of the gift ingredients. Protein-rich almonds (**ABOVE**) keep everyone's minds on the tasks at hand. Pour roasted almonds into a sealable plastic bag and sprinkle in sea salt and powdered honey. Shake until the nuts are coated, then serve. Cranberry fizz (cranberry juice mixed with seltzer water) is a refreshing sipper in vintage-looking jelly jars (**RIGHT**). Spike it with vodka if desired.

OPPOSITE: Top slices of fresh-baked baguette with a smear of goat cheese and fig jam or fresh figs and honey. Bake up some shortbread rounds and pair with jalapeño jelly for a palate kicker.

HOW TO) VANILLA VODKA

WHAT YOU'LL NEED: 3 to 5 whole vanilla beans, vodka, glass jar with tight-fitting lid, such as this recycled water jar or Mason jar

STEP BY STEP:

ONE: Place the vanilla beans in the jar. Cover completely with vodka.

TWO: Top with pretty linen cover secured with twine or ribbon. Let the recipient know that it will reach full flavor in two months. After that, it lasts for years if you top it off with fresh vodka and give it a good shake periodically. Mix it into baked goods or in mixed drinks.

Tie on a tag with a delicious cocktail recipe: 1 part vanilla vodka, 1 part creme de cacao, 1 part cream. Shake with ice and serve dusted with chocolate shavings.

PRESERVED LEMONS

WHAT YOU'LL NEED: 4–5 whole lemons, 6 sprigs fresh dill weed or 3 to 4 sprigs fresh thyme, 3 to 4 leaves fresh bay leaves, 4 peeled garlic cloves, 1⅔ cups white wine vinegar, 1 tablespoon salt

STEP BY STEP:

ONE: Clean lemons and remove stems if necessary. In a large saucepan, cook lemons in boiling water for 1 minute. Drain and dry the lemons with a paper towel. Cut lemons in ¼-inch thick slices.

TWO: Pack lemons with dill or thyme, bay leaves, and garlic into a sterilized wide mouth jar. In the same saucepan, heat vinegar with salt just to boiling. Let cool.

THREE: Pour vinegar mixture over lemons in the jar. Add more vinegar to cover lemons if necessary. Refrigerate 2–3 weeks or longer.

Use the vinegar to flavor salad dressings and marinades. Use the lemons or just their peels in sauces or to top fish.

WARM AND *Wooly*

ALLOW WINTER TO WRAP YOU IN THE WARMTH OF THE FESTIVE SEASON.

Woolen sweaters and intricate snowflakes announce the arrival of winter.

$\mathcal{W}inter$ $comes$ $early$ in Matthew's neck of the woods, so as soon as the Thanksgiving dishes are washed and put away, out come gentle nods to the season. For those like Matthew, who favor a more subtle approach to holiday decorating, digging through trunks for packed-away woolen sweaters, scarves, and blankets often yields all that is needed to stylishly layer a bright sunroom. Woolen items can be collected from around the house or purchased for a song from thrift shops and flea markets. Look for knitted treasures that have small holes from years of wear. Minor imperfections and discoloring can be cut away and sleeves, cuffs, and collars can be put to use as cozies for jars, lamps, and dishes. Slip a cable-knit sweater over a humble side chair and show off your knitting skills by making fuzzy slippers to tuck tiny presents in. The best part? This wintry décor can be left out long past the holidays for months of cozy style.

Shimmering touches add sparkle to a casual mix of weathered wood and knitted embellishments. A vintage candelabrum (ABOVE, LEFT) casts a warm, flickering glow. Hang festive cardboard ornaments—that have been brushed with Mod Podge® and dusted with glitter—on doorknobs, chairs, and hooks (ABOVE, RIGHT).

A spindly wire tree shows off shiny ornaments in cool blues and silvers, but a wool pennant garland and a gingerbread man dressed in a scarf are warm notes.

cuddle bunny

A stuffed bunny, fashioned from an old sweater, is a light sewing project that can be created in multiples for sweetly simple gifts for children and/or the young at heart. Allow your imagination to guide your stuffed animal designs. Cut out a pocket shape from the sweater and stitch it to the front of the bunny. Fill it with small gifts or treats and add a simple face using embroidery floss.

divine details

Special touches offer up festive flair. **1.** A pewter bowl is filled with an assortment of glass ornaments. Nestle in a string of beaded garland for extra sparkle. **2.** A vintage iron snowflake rests against a window, allowing the sun's rays to highlight its detailed form. **3.** A store-bought cookie is secured to a tiny package using simple twine. **4.** Stitch the edges of a thrift-store scarf together and fill it with buckwheat hulls to create a serviceable draft dodger. Sew on vintage buttons for old-school charm.

toasty warm

With a little creativity and some basic knitting skills you can make an abundance of projects from a few woolen pieces. **1.** Use your favorite slipper pattern to create these fuzzy foot warmers. Filled with small trinkets, they are charming stand-ins for more predictable stockings. **2.** Set up welcoming knitting station with caddies for yarns and needles, as well as drinks kept warm in a knit cozy. **3.** Use an old sweater to make wintry stockings. Stitch the two sides together and trim it with a fabric cuff that has been stenciled in a snowflake pattern.

OPPOSITE: Make a cozy yarn ball container to hold supplies close by. Cut the sleeve from a tired sweater and slide it over a glass jar. Place a current yarn ball on top and tuck in necessary needles.

HOW TO TINY WOOLEN HAT

WHAT YOU'LL NEED: Gray wool yarn (30–40 pieces of 10-inch lengths), a ring cut from a wrapping paper roll or paper towel tube (about ½- to ¾- inches wide), scissors

STEP BY STEP:

ONE: Double each piece of yarn and slip the loop end through the ring. Pull both ends through the loop and tighten them up, pulling snugly but not too tight.

TWO: Work the yarn pieces closely together to completely fill in the ring, ensuring that no cardboard is showing.

THREE: When the ring is fully covered, gather all of the yarn ends and tie them tightly with another piece of yarn.

FOUR: Trim the loose ends with sharp scissors to form a pompom on top. Make several to slip over the covers of bottled honey, maple syrup, herbal extracts, or even wine.

The tiny hats can be placed over the tops of new, unused candles for charming hostess gifts.

Fill a wee bottle with peppermint schnapps
to add to tea or to flavor hot cocoa.

Crafting a
WOOLPENNANT

What you'll need:

- ○ One piece of cardstock paper for the triangle template
- ○ Old pre-shrunken sweater
- ○ Micro-tip scissors or very pointy, sharp scissors
- ○ Yarn cut to the desired length for the garland
- ○ Clear adhesive tape

ONE: Cut a standard triangle (4-inch wide x 4¾-inch length template from the cardstock or a piece of recycled cardboard. Lay the sweater flat and place the cardboard template on top. Use scissors to cut around the template until you have 8 triangles; cut out more if you wish to make a longer garland.

TWO: If the sweater is wrinkled or puckered, use a steam iron to flatten each triangle before hanging. Using micro-tip scissors, cut two small slits approximately ½-inch from the top and ½-inch from the side of each triangle. Wrap a piece of tape around the end of the yarn so it will easily glide through the slits in the sweater.

THREE: Weave the yarn through the triangles as shown above. Tie a tassel at each end of the garland for a finishing flourish.

To ready a sweater for this no-sew craft, first wash it in hot water and dry it on high heat. This shrinks the fibers so they won't fray and unravel when you cut the triangles.

WHAT YOU'LL NEED: A snowflake template (find on page 159 and at HolidayWithMatthewMead.com), sharp pencil, scissors, ruler or straight edge, white paint pen, plant pot, sturdy linen fabric

STEP BY STEP:

ONE: Cut out the snowflake template and place it on the object you wish to stencil. At the center of the snowflake design, use a sharp pencil to poke a hole through the paper onto the surface to be stencilled, creating the center mark. Use the white paint pen to make tiny marks at the points of each snowflake. Lift the template away.

TWO: Line up a ruler or straight edge from the painted dots to the center mark. Draw a line to connect the dots to it.

THREE: Follow the template as a guide and fill in the snowflake details by hand using the paint pen.

FOUR: Use the snowflake template to create a variety of wintry projects. Here, fabric yardage from a thrift store offers is stitched into a runner and embellished with the snowflake detailing.

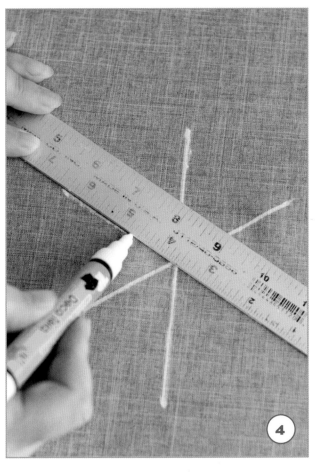

Both projects can be beautifully created using recycled materials. Thrift shop fabrics and recycled plant pots from your potting shed allow you to create projects on a dime.

FIVE: Follow step three to fill in the snowflake design using the white paint pen.

SIX: After filling in the details, allow the fabric to dry overnight before using.

Christmas ON THE FARM

MATTHEW VISITS THE COUNTRY—AND A HOUSE ROOTED IN SIMPLICITY.

He captures the sights and scents of a holiday celebrated the old-fashioned way.

On top of a hill in rural New Hampshire, Sandy and Jim Gorman celebrate life on a country lane. Their bow-roof Cape Cod-style house is nestled in the woods, surrounded by gardens and boxwood trees as if it belongs on the pages of a storybook. When I met Sandy at her antiques booth at a local shop years ago, I loved her selection and carted home loads of the furnishings and accessories she offered. I knew before I ever saw her home that it would be a wonderful place to experience at the holidays.

Sandy admires simplicity in all its romantic forms, from painted country cupboards to hand-knit blankets to brown-paper packages truly tied with string. "I like uncluttered decorating scenarios and using items from nature," she told me. Her Christmas trees are adorned only with small white lights. Hurricane candles perch on windowsills. Fresh greens, pinecones, and rose hips are spread throughout the house. It was an inspiring place to photograph, but even more, it was a comforting, welcoming place to enjoy a slower, more thoughtful pace.

One of Sandy Gorman's trees is a feathery hemlock in a vintage stand, which she enjoys au naturel (ABOVE). A shapely glass pendant adds dimmable light to complement the candles (BOTTOM LEFT). Garden statues are brought inside to grace tabletops (BOTTOM CENTER). A glass light shade on a pewter plate becomes a candleholder (BOTTOM RIGHT).

A long industrial farm table spans two windows and holds focal point items, including a Scotch pine branch in an antique crock.

it's a wrap

Sandy's office space pulls second shift this time of year as a room for wrapping gifts. **1.** A citrus wreath is a project she's likely to tackle in this hardworking space. Instead of hanging it predictably on the front door, she enjoys the aroma indoors. You'll find instructions for how to make it on page 100.
2. Sandy collects yarn in neutral shades and natural fibers to make all kinds of knitted items, such as wooly lavender sachets. **3.** Natural elements, such as pinecones and feathers, make elegant gift toppers secured with vintage string or jute ribbon.

OPPOSITE: She keeps the room well stocked with supplies, and she can close it off from view when it's not in use. A tin-topped table is a durable work surface.

like the Warmth of
the Sun
And the light of
the day
May the luck of
the Irish
Shine bright on
your way

Thank
you
For
my ball
Love
Nova

SHY RABBIT FARM
SHY RABBIT FARM
SHY RABBIT FARM

ever presents

Everywhere I set up my camera in Sandy's house, I was struck by yet another picturesque vignette that captured the spirit of the season. Many of her displays include packages and gifts she will bestow on friends and family. "Most of my gifts are handmade," she says. "Everyone receives some jam, knit scarves, mittens, and hats, or something sewn." Sandy's kitchen is always churning out jars of tasty preserves (**RIGHT**) or zesty herbal vinegars.

Just as in her decorating, Sandy's kitchen preparations are guided by simplicity. "I like to try new and interesting recipes that I can prepare ahead," she says. She makes a few different kinds of cookies, "one of which is always a recipe passed down from my grandmother." A selection of sweets and savories are casually laid out on a serve board in the dining room (**BOTTOM LEFT**). Mini tarts are filled with her blueberry jam (**BOTTOM RIGHT**).

OPPOSITE: "The food is mostly about presentation and making people feel comfortable," she says. When she offers treats, she relies on vintage ironstone, handmade pottery, metal trays, wooden cutting boards, cake stands, and natural elements. A tall piece of slate conveys favorite thoughts.

freshly picked

Sandy prefers to decorate with items found in nature, including bushels of citrus fruits, which reach their flavorful peak at this time of year. They add subtle color and texture, as well as appetizing fragrance. In the spacious entry, Sandy greets guests with a stack of gifts and a bowl of fruit. A wreath calls attention to a beloved cupboard.

OPPOSITE: Here, the fruit is arrayed with seeded eucalyptus on a stack of old nickel pastry stands. "I start decorating about two weeks before Christmas, so everything feels fresh and exciting," she says.

dinner invitation

Sandy's dining table is a delight for the eye and beckons guests to come sit for a lengthy meal. Creamy Wedgwood plates mix with old pewter cups and handmade glassware on a delightfully rumpled linen runner (**RIGHT**). Craft paper envelopes hold vintage silverware for each guest (**ABOVE**).

OPPOSITE: White walls and spare, graphic adornment in the dining room keep the focus on the warm, welcoming table. It glows in the light of a rustic chandelier and several votive candles down the middle of the table.

Crafting a
CITRUSCENTERPIECE

What you'll need:

- ○ Citrus fruit, such as lemons, oranges, tangerines, kumquats, and limes
- ○ Bamboo skewer
- ○ Whole cloves
- ○ Large shallow vessel, such as a platter, tray, or bowl
- ○ Fresh fragrant greens, such as pine and bay leaves

TWO: Insert whole cloves into the holes.

THREE: Vary the designs from one fruit to the next to create an interesting array.

OPPOSITE: Nestle the fruit in a shallow container, which allows the most aroma to circulate into the room. Tuck in pinecones and greens to enhance the look and scent.

ONE: Poke holes through the rind of the fruit, taking care to pierce in straight, even lines to form patterns.

This arrangement will grow more fragrant over a number of days. Store it in the refrigerator at night to help it last longer.

HOW TO CITRUS WREATH

WHAT YOU'LL NEED: Fresh green wreath; whole citrus fruits, such as lemons, Meyer lemons, oranges, and tangerines; bamboo skewers; green floral wire; scissors

STEP BY STEP:

ONE: Poke a skewer straight through a whole fruit to make a path for the floral wire.

TWO: Thread the floral wire through the path, letting 3–4 inches extend on either side of the fruit. Cut off excess wire.

THREE: Pick a spot on the wreath to attach the fruit, and then bend the wire ends around either side of the wreath form, hiding the wire under leaves if possible. On the back of the wreath, twist the wire ends together.

For interest, vary the direction the fruits face so some show smooth sides and some show bumpy navels.

Matthew Mead

OUTDOOR
Décor

HERE ARE TEN FESTIVE IDEAS TO DECK YOUR HOUSE OR GIVE AS GIFTS.

Matthew Mead

Engage the spirit of the season with a porch party for carolers.

The image of an ideal

Christmas that most of us have is inspired by Currier & Ives prints or Norman Rockwell paintings of old New England homes, farms, and streets dusted with a thick layer of sparkling white snow. When we stored away these images, it was because they connoted serenity, comfort, family, and simplicity.

While the snowfall and generations-old buildings may not be reality for everyone, they are for Matthew. He makes the most of his picturesque New Hampshire setting, using early-American architecture and northern-climate foliage to create decorating projects that we can re-create for our far-flung homes.

These truly traditional holiday ideas were created for the porches, doors, and grounds of the historic Kimball-Jenkins estate in Concord, New Hampshire, which Matthew photographed during a particularly gorgeous snowfall last year. But the ideas are universal: Beckon neighbors to your home with a dessert party set up on the porch, hang a fragrant wreath on the front door as a sign of appreciation for the fleeting season, or lovingly pack a basket of goodies to present to dear friends. No matter where you live, the priorities of the season—as prompted by those idyllic images—are the same.

The Kimball-Jenkins estate (ABOVE) was once the home of a prominent Concord, New Hampshire, family, and is now a nationally recognized school of art and popular site for weddings and events. The red brick exterior of the carriage house pictured above, inspired Matthew's choice of deep red roses for small tabletop bouquets (RIGHT), wreaths, and large urn arrangements. Leaving a basket of goodies at someone's doorstep (OPPOSITE) is a singular gift-giving pleasure. Matthew lined a this ample basket with a Turkey red damask tablecloth, then tucked in seasonal fruits, cakes from a local bakery, and small gifts. A bottle of wine is wrapped in a matching napkin.

flower power

Fresh greens and bold flowers make an impact on curb appeal. Tall arrangements (**OPPOSITE**) are visible from the street, and small pots (**ABOVE**) lined up front steps or placed next to the door are intimately inviting.

OPPOSITE: For a large, focal point arrangement, Matthew filled a cast-iron garden urn with a vivid green, red, and white arrangement. The greens are boxwood and arborvitae branches, snipped from bushes near his house, and seeded eucalyptus from the florist. The white hydrangea is echoed by the edges of variegated euonymus branches. Punches of red come from hypericum berries, large variegated red roses, and smaller spray roses.

sweets appeal

Carolers used to be a common sight in neighborhoods during the holiday season. People would be sure to have something warm to drink and a bite to eat to greet the serenaders. You can keep up a portion of that tradition by inviting neighbors to stop by your porch one evening for holiday cheer and tasty treats like these cream-filled horns (**BELOW**) from the pastry shop.

OPPOSITE: A hot cocoa bar with tempting additions, including whipped cream, marshmallows, and ladyfingers, is also welcome on a chilly night.

small takes

These quick-and-easy ideas give you a seasonal look in a flash. **1.** For this door hanger, spruce up a pair of old skates with a coat of spray paint. Stuff the insides with newspaper, but leave room in the ankle for stems of greens and berries. Place the stems in water-picks first if you want the arrangement to last longer than a few days. **2.** Tie twine to the stems of three large pinecones (which you can scavenge or purchase at a crafts store), then add a ribbon bow. Hot-glue on greens and flowers as you wish. **3.** Hot-glue the seeds of a pine cone into a circle and add a star anise to the top and a small pinecone to the bottom. The wee wreath can dress a window, hang on a doorknocker, or tuck into a flower arrangement.

OPPOSITE: Invite your feathered friends to your home with this outdoor tree ornament. Purchase a birdseed-covered star from the grocery or hardware store and punch a hole in the top. Tie twine though the hole to secure it to a branch, and tie on a rose, too, for pretty color.

Crafting a
YULETIDE BUNDLE

What you'll need:

- ❍ Three birch logs, or another log with attractive bark
- ❍ Twine
- ❍ 1 yard satin ribbon
- ❍ Aromatic natural embellishments, such as cinnamon sticks, nutmeg, and whole star anise

ONE: Gather your supplies, which can all be purchased at a crafts store, grocery store, or gathered from the yard. Matthew used long cinnamon, pinecones, nutmeg, sprigs of spruce, yew, arborvitae, and seeded eucalyptus, and a stem of hypericum berries.

TWO: Cluster the logs together, and tie securely around the middle with twine.

THREE: Conceal the twine with a pretty bow tied from 1-inch satin ribbon.

FOUR: Using the trailing ends of the ribbon, tie in cinnamon sticks, berries, and sprigs of greens. Spray them with water to keep them fresh and fragrant. Hot-glue on nutmeg and star anise as desired.

After the bow is removed, the twine-bound logs and natural decorations can be burned to release exotic seasonal fragrances.

ROSY WREATH

WHAT YOU'LL NEED: Evergreen wreath, pinecones in various sizes, floral wire, wire cutters, hot-glue gun, water picks from the crafts store, fresh red roses

STEP BY STEP:

ONE: Lay out your supplies. Cut lengths of floral wire to wrap around pinecones. To attach them to the wreath, twist the loose ends around the wreath form, or a clump of greens.

TWO: Add smaller elements, such as tiny pinecones or sprigs of berries using a hot-glue gun.

THREE: Finally, tuck in bright flowers. Snip the stems short and tuck them into water-filled picks. To secure the picks, wedge the tips into the wreath form, and secure with hot glue if necessary.

You can embellish a store-bought wreath in minutes, giving it a personally unique and fresh look.

Green GOLD

EASY-TO-FIND CLIPPINGS MAKE BUDGET-FRIENDLY DÉCOR.

Dip into a jackpot of readily available greenery—gather it on a walk or snip it from the yard—for these festive DIY accents.

This time of year, floral and garden shops display a bounty of mouth-watering holiday arrangements. Bringing one home can be a lovely splurge, but sprinkling the fragrance and allure of seasonal greenery room to room can be hard on the pocketbook—unless you turn to humble evergreen landscaping plants as fodder. No need to rely on exotic materials when you can obtain leaves with texture and color variation—the key elements in a successful floral arrangement—right out the door.

Before you begin, take an inventory walk. Chances are, you or your willing neighbors have yew bushes, holly, boxwood, or pachysandra in their yards. Not sure? Look online for pictures of evergreen leaves. Fill a bucket with cool water and ask permission to snip some branches.

At home, a table on the porch or deck, or a small corner of the garage will be your studio. Gather basic supplies at the crafts store, including floral foam shapes, wire, and wreath forms. Then follow Matthew's lead by using these inspiring images and step-by-step instructions to create your own gorgeous flourishes.

Spread newspaper to protect your work surface. Lisa Bisson, who created these projects, suggests dividing supplies into separate water-filled containers so you can quickly assess them for color (deep green to chartreuse) and form (spiky, smooth, or drapey).

birds of a feather

Matthew combined greenery with small bird statues (LEFT). If you have a collection of garden figurines, small Santas, or vintage ornaments, work items into the displays for a meaningful look. The footed urn (BELOW) is shallow enough for a shelf or mantel. Matthew echoed the lines of the container, anchoring stiff branches of yew, holly, and variegated euonymus in a foam base to form an arc shape.

OPPOSITE: Atop a stone pedestal, Matthew placed a dove figure under the top of a topiary form, and the melding of rustic objects takes on an elegant look. For the nest, he wove yew, clumps of dried moss from the crafts store, and holly branches through the wire.

room by room

Once you've gathered supplies and practiced basic methods for arranging branches, you can play with placement and materials. For example, after you cover foam spheres in short snippets of greens—pale greens for one and dark leaves for another), you can place them atop a candlestick to create a topiary for the powder room sink (ABOVE, LEFT), or in a shallow bowl as a dining table centerpiece (RIGHT). Some decorations can be quite simple: Use six leftover branches to form a spray with a ribbon bow, and use them to hang up a decorative plaque or holiday plate (ABOVE, RIGHT).

OPPOSITE: Matthew placed a foam-filled glass bowl in this old candleholder, filled it with various branches, and hung it from a peg in his dining room. When placing arrangements throughout the house, look for spots high, low, and off the beaten path. A wreath hanging over the bed, or a basket of branches on the floor next to the family room sofa are unexpected spots for festive color.

Crafting a
LEAFYTOPIARY

What you'll need:

- ○ Floral foam in a cone shape
- ○ Water-filled bucket in which the foam shape can be submerged
- ○ Pachysandra snippets
- ○ A base, such as an urn, upside down vase, or a thick candlestick

ONE: Place the foam cone in the bucket of water and let soak until fully saturated.

TWO: Place the cone on a flat work surface, and begin covering with short snippets of pachysandra, an evergreen shrub with grass-green glossy leaves in a starburst shape. The leaves have a stiff stem, which is ideal for inserting in the foam.

THREE: Cover the top of the cone with smaller leaves, and choose larger ones as you work down to the base. Leave no spots of foam cone exposed.

The cone looks elegant settled on a sculptural base, such as this old brass lamp base. You could also use another flea-market-find, such as a trophy cup or urn, or just use your favorite large candlestick.

MULTI-COLOR SPHERE

WHAT YOU'LL NEED: Grapevine ball from the crafts store floral aisle; short branches of yew, euonymus, holly, juniper, and arborvitae; dried salal leaves (also called lemon leaves); 1-inch diameter straight stick; floral foam; dried moss; heavy vessel, such as a metal urn or stone vase

STEP BY STEP:

ONE: Fill the vessel with floral foam, and plunge one end of the straight stick into the center of the foam, until it's anchored. Cover the foam with dried moss. Skewer the grapevine ball on top of the exposed end of the stick.

TWO: Cover the ball in various snippets and leaves. Work from one side of the ball to the other, filling in empty spots as you go. Cluster three or four of the same green or leaf together for each spot. Alternate specimens as you go, so colors and textures are separate.

Instead of using several different-color greens, you can cover the spheres with just one specimen type for an impactful look called pavé. Insert the snippets until covered, then trim to even lengths when finished.

To create a symmetrical arrangement on a buffet, make twin topiaries. Or, for a pleasing grouping to put in the middle of a coffee or dining table, make an odd number, such as three, and vary the texture and color of the greens for interest.

RAD *Plaid*

GREET GUESTS WITH A FRESH TAKE ON TARTAN.

Tradition with a twist makes for a grand entrance.

Lighten up the tradition

of plaid at Christmas with fun, doable projects that can enliven any room in your house. Starting at the very beginning, a serviceable but stylish entryway receives some Highland charm via colorful plaid décor, blankets, and holiday trinkets. Steal an old shirt from grandpa or visit a local thrift shop or two for shirts you won't mind cutting into sections to scan on your home computer or at the copy center. Tiny trees enliven even the most utilitarian corner. Place a feather tree in an iron urn (OPPOSITE) and adorn with ornaments and live pinecones. Layer in sprigs of fragrant evergreens, and hang boughs—gathered in a bunch and secured with ribbon—from hooks and doorknobs. Drape tartan blankets over coat hooks (RIGHT) so visitors can easily grab one to ward off the winter chill after a day spent building snowmen, ice skating, or simply enjoying the winter sun.

A large cider ball (BELOW), spray-painted red and filled with balsam evergreen needles or cedar chips, makes a fragrant moth chaser to hang amongst winter coats, woolens, and blankets.

Even the tight spaces of an entry hall or mudroom can have room for a small tree. For a live specimen, choose a dwarf spruce or potted boxwood. For a tree you can reuse year to year, choose a wire tree, such as this one, which can be displayed in any heavy vessel then folded up to be stored.

flickering light

Glass hurricanes wrapped in plaid papers (**BELOW**) announce the tartan theme. Use double-stick tape to affix the paper to the outside of the glass, and pop in a real or battery-operated candle.

OPPOSITE: From boots, blankets, and baskets to skis, snow shoes, and skates, just about anything wintry or sporty will look great as purposeful props in a welcoming mudroom. Use a metal tray to stylishly corral dripping winter boots, and tuck mittens and hats in stacked baskets.

basic beauties

1. A few pleats and folds transform paper into holiday ornaments. Hang them in threes on the wall, or glue on a photo of the family pet for a personalized keepsake. **2.** Stylish boots inject the space with a robust, wintry nod. **3.** A twig basket becomes a woodland forest: Fill it with moss and tiny bottle-brush trees, and place it next to a small stack of firewood. **4.** A pinecone tree nestles nicely into an old, red fireplace ash pot.

Update a tiny holiday house by using découpage medium to cover it in plaid paper.

grab and go

A wooden tray lined with plaid paper (**BELOW**) is the perfect spot to display stacks of freshly baked cookies that can serve as take-away treats when friends and family stop by for a holiday visit. Shortbread cookies molded into Scottie dog shapes (**RIGHT**) fit the highlands mood. Give them as gifts or hang them as decorations from strips of plaid fabric.

OPPOSITE: Nothing is more appealing than a traditionally decorated spruce tree that emphasizes the main hues in the plaid patterns. Branches of variegated and chartreuse greenery inject verdant color, and assorted red ornaments are regal touches.

Crafting a
PLAIDCARDHOLDER

What you'll need:

- ○ 1½ yards of tartan/plaid ribbon
- ○ Adhesive putty
- ○ Scissors
- ○ Holiday greeting cards
- ○ Push pin

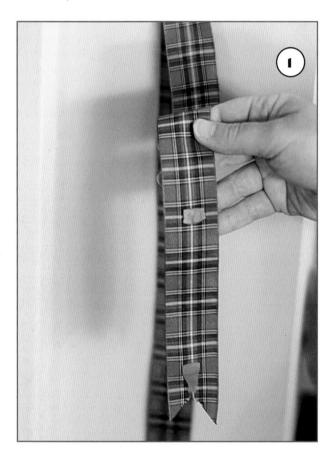

ONE: Cut off 8 inches from the ribbon to make the ribbon topper and set aside. Fold the remaining length of ribbon in half and press small pieces of adhesive putty to the front of the top ribbon. Space the pieces to reflect the size of the cards to be displayed.

TWO: Fold the 8-inch piece of ribbon in half and spread it apart a little to create the topper. Hold the ribbon topper firmly at the center and use a push pin to secure all of the ribbon pieces to the wall.

THREE: Apply small pieces of adhesive putty to the backs of each greeting card and line up the putty on the back of the cards with the putty pieces on the front of the ribbon. Press to secure.

Use this idea throughout the year: Any festive ribbon can show off birthday or anniversary greetings. Use pale blue or pink to display cards congratulating you on a new baby.

HOW TO — PINECONE WREATH

WHAT YOU'LL NEED: Wooden oval frame from the crafts store, medium and small pinecones, chestnuts, hot glue gun and glue sticks, small picture hanger

STEP BY STEP:

ONE: Use a hot glue gun to adhere a single layer of evenly-sized pinecones to the base of the oval.

TWO: Add dimension to the wreath by gluing on additional pinecones in different sizes and shapes, filling in any bare spots.

THREE: Finish by gluing the chestnuts to the wreath in a random fashion. Secure the picture hanger to the back of the oval form and hang the wreath on a door or wall.

Head outdoors for a nature walk to gather a variety of pinecones before the snow flies.

Crafting a
PLAIDWRAP

What you'll need:

- ○ Plaid shirt or fabric
- ○ Scissors
- ○ Candle votives
- ○ Matchboxes
- ○ Double-stick tape

Once you have created the paper it can be used for a variety of holiday projects.

ONE: Collect an assortment of size large or extra-large plaid shirts from the thrift store.

TWO: Make plaid wrap by cutting out the back of the shirts or use plaid fabric. Scan or copy the plaid fabric cuttings at a copy center.

THREE: Apply double-stick tape to the back of the papers and wrap around candle holders to make decorative votives and pillars, or glue the paper onto matchboxes (OPPOSITE) for pretty, seasonal hostess gifts.

PURE WINTER *Style*

Photos by Kindra Clineff

DESIGNER TERRY JOHN WOODS WELCOMES US TO HIS SERENE VERMONT HOME.

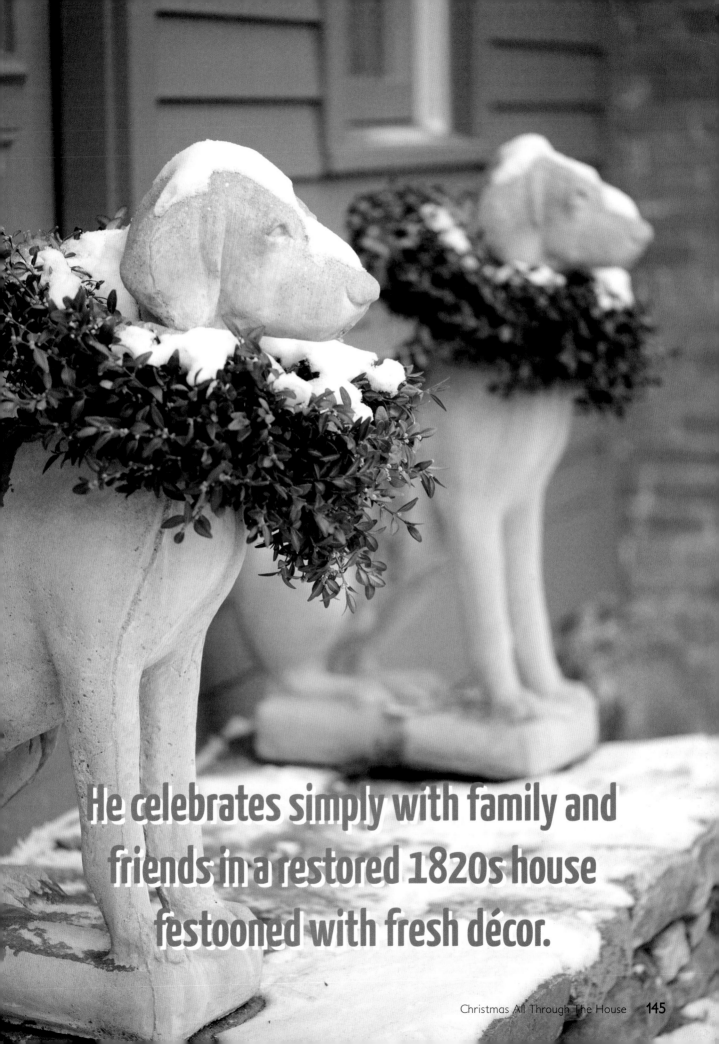

He celebrates simply with family and friends in a restored 1820s house festooned with fresh décor.

Forlorn and nearly condemned,

the brick parsonage in central Vermont, had little going for it apart from its genuine Federal-style lines. Designer and author Terry John Woods and his partner Dale West were undaunted by the dingy trim, brocade wallpaper, and worn walnut floors. Terry knew that with the large windows and high ceilings, the house could be made to feel bright, open, and airy. After two years of painstaking restoration work ("I saved every piece of old glass and inch of broken plaster," he says) Terry saw his vision complete. Today, the home is renewed and thriving. And when the Christmas season arrives, the house really comes alive, as if it had lain in wait just to welcome people back again at this special time. All Terry has to do is add boughs of Scotch pine and balsam clipped from the property and throw open the doors to family and friends. The house does the rest.

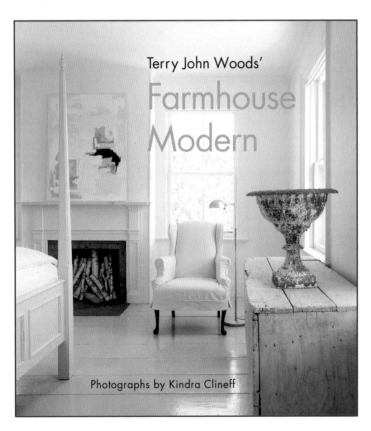

Terry John Woods and photographer Kindra Clineff captured the seasonal magic of his Vermont house in their new book, *Terry John Woods' Farmhouse Modern* (2013; Stewart, Tabori & Chang), which chronicles the updated style of historic homes throughout New England.

"I don't like pristine," Terry says. A long-time collector, he has winnowed down his interests to a few style categories and prefers tarnished silver candlesticks and chipped English ironstone to perfect specimens. "When I buy a piece, I look for distressing because it's texture," he says.

style simplified

White furnishings join whitewashed walls and trim for clean-feeling spaces. **1.** A French rusty metal table holds a bouquet of branches and a dish of paperwhite bulbs. Fresh cut branches provide "the aroma and feel of a natural Christmas," he says. **2.** A wide shallow cabinet in the hall becomes a bar and buffet during informal holiday gatherings. "We set out hors d'oeuvres and drinks, and people just mill throughout the house," he says. **3.** A tall Palladian window propped on the mantel takes advantage of nearly 10-foot ceilings. "I like to bring the eye up and make things soar," Terry says. On the floor, one of the sap buckets Terry's father once used to tap trees on their farm holds branches.

OPPOSITE: When he strings large old-fashioned white bulbs on a sparse tree, Terry plugs them into dimmers. "It's a more natural look than that abrasive light shining through," he says. "It creates such an atmosphere." An avid squirrel watcher, Tyler, the couple's golden retriever, appreciates that the house's restored windows are left uncovered and open to the view.

less means more

A few large arrangements are an unfussy way to convey the holiday spirit. A large tray of greens surrounds folk art dove sculptures (**ABOVE**), and a hanging print becomes festive with a crown of boxwood branches and a row of potted mini poinsettia (**BELOW**). Terry sticks to greens with dark foliage, which stand out in contrast to the light interiors and furnishings.

case study

A primitive folk-art horse sits atop a pie safe wearing a large pine wreath, which Terry purchases from a local shop. Featuring the wreath as part of such a quiet arrangement boosts its stature, so no extra lights or shiny embellishments are needed.

subtle sparkle

Shiny silver ball ornaments make a fetching scene with a cement garden sculpture and painted wood croquet balls. Though you could say his decorating is limited to only one color—white—Terry begs to differ: "My color is texture," he says. The palette stretches from pale gray to natural wood, and the editing serves to amplify each piece's lines as well as its unique finish, material, and patina.

single moments

In a home that is decorated with a light hand, each composed vignette becomes more notable: **1.** A concrete dog sculpture wears a jolly wreath of boxwood. You'll find instructions for making the wreath on page 156. **2.** By clustering slender candlesticks together, they take on a larger presence. A banner printed with words of the season speaks volumes. **3.** Hyacinths bulbs are potted in an English pudding mold. **4.** A small wreath draws attention to artwork.

collected look

Terry puts his collections to use. **1.** A transferware compote holds forced paperwhite bulbs rooting in a collection of beach rocks. **2.** A vintage tea towel can be used as a pretty cuff for amaryllis in a vase. **3.** Terry unifies mismatched upholstery pieces of every ilk and era with custom slipcovers sewn from painter's drop cloths he buys at the hardware store. "Over time, they get a really soft linen feel," he says. One of the bears he designs for TerryJohnWoods.com rests on the settee in his Vermont studio.

OPPOSITE: Smooth, shapely ironstone pitchers are set off by the spiky needles of Scotch pine branches, which Terry cuts from trees on the property. He looks for ones with pinecones attached.

HOW TO BOXWOOD WREATH

WHAT YOU'LL NEED: Boxwood branches and loose boxwood leaves, green floral tape, green floral wire, scissors

STEP BY STEP:

ONE: Gather your supplies. The larger loose boxwood leaves are nice to mix in with the smaller leaves on the branches. If you don't have boxwood, you can use any greenery to make this wreath, including pine, pachysandra, and seeded eucalyptus.

TWO: Determine the wreath size, and then cut the floral wire to length. Starting at one end, wrap the tape as seen in the photo. As you wrap, add branches of greens.

THREE: Overlap the branches and intersperse leaves as you work down the wire with the tape.

FOUR: As you complete the circle, plan how you'll finish it. At the end, choose a bushy snippet that will hide the final coil of tape.

These small wreaths have myriad uses—hang them from stair banisters, at the top of stockings, or around garden statuary.

Resources

Cake and Cookie Decorating

The Baker's Kitchen
TheBakersKitchen.net

Chandlers Cake and Candy Supplies
ChandlersCakeandCandy.com

Chef Tools Network, Inc
ChefTools.com

Fancy Flours
FancyFlours.com

Garnish
ThinkGarnish.com/store

Wilton
Wilton.com

Holiday Entertaining

Fish's Eddy
FishsEddy.com

Grenon Trading Co.
276 Route 101
Bedford, NH 03110
603/472-3946

Nature Crafts Supplies

Attar Herbs and Spices
AttarHerbs.com

Lynch Creek Farm
LynchCreekWreaths.com

Maine Wreath Company
MaineWreathCo.com

Nature's Pressed Flowers
NaturesPressed.com

Wrapping Papers and Party Supplies

Paper Mart
PaperMart.com

Paper Source
Paper-Source.com

Pearl River, Inc.
PearlRiver.com

PIKKU
PIKKUwares.com

Red River Paper
RedRiverCatalog.com

Templates and Recipes

HolidayWithMatthewMead.com

Crafts

A.C. Moore Arts & Crafts
ACMoore.com

Anything In Stained Glass
AnythingInStainedGlass.com

Create For Less
CreateForLess.com

Fiskars
Fiskars.com

JoAnn Fabric and Craft Stores
JoAnn.com

June Tailor, Inc.
JuneTailor.com

Michaels Stores
Michaels.com

Home Décor

Bethany Lowe
BethanyLowe.com

Crate & Barrel
CrateAndBarrel.com

Janna Lufkin
RawMaterialDesign.com

Macy's
Macys.com

Matthew Mead Collection
Etsy.com/Shop/MatthewMeadVintage

Pier 1 Imports
Pier1.com

Target
Target.com

Terry John Woods
TerryJohnWoods.com

TJX Companies
HomeGoods.com
TJMaxx.com
MarshallsOnline.com

West Elm
WestElm.com

Office Supplies

The Container Store
ContainerStore.com

Staples
Staples.com

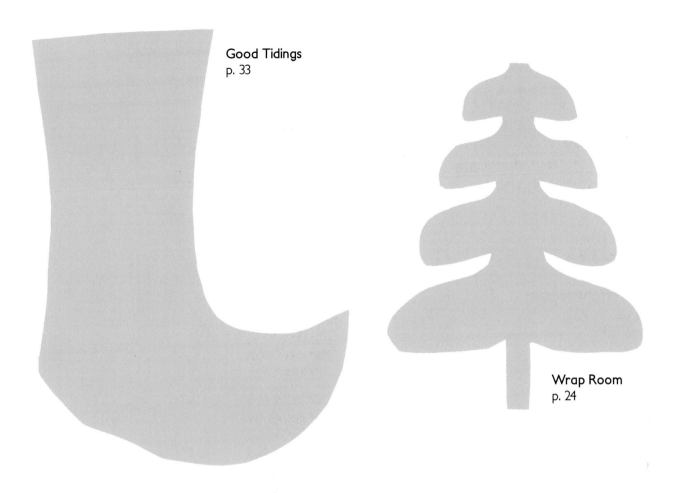

Good Tidings
p. 33

Wrap Room
p. 24

Warm and Wooly
p. 82

Warm and Wooly
p. 84

knee high in Christmas

Got a sec? For a cinch-to-make stairway decoration or door hanger, choose a ready-made felt stocking and sturdy scrapbook stickers in shades of red and white. Affix the embellishments with their adhesive backing so you can quickly change and personalize them year to year. Or, use the stocking as a gift package topper, and make the decorations permanent with little dots of fabric glue.